My Conversations with AI

Volume 2

Incredible Fantasy Cliff Houses ???

A SHORT PICTURE STUDY

ETIENNE LUTHER

1

Artificial Intelligence

By now, most of you have seen, heard, or read about the latest human technological breakthroughs based on Artificial Intelligence, more commonly known as "AI."

When I first began researching AI, it was purely out of fear. I initially felt this new "make-believe" intelligence was a fad or phase and would die a quiet death like so many other "fads" have done. Still, I secretly felt unnerved that a bunch of zeros and ones placed in various orders could actually think for itself, sometimes better and more efficiently than human beings.

However, as the past few years have progressed, I've noted an ever-increasing reliance upon AI to do just about anything a human can, including thinking of new ideas and creating new things. So, I've determined that AI is not going away.

I have researched and reviewed several amazing things that could have only been created using this new type of technology. Although I am still a little squeamish when I experience some of the results of this endeavor, my mind is opened to previously unimaginable possibilities and discoveries based on the results of my studies.

Therefore, as an author of words and creator in the visual arts, I have decided that instead of being afraid and running from AI, I should stop, turn, and try to embrace it and use it as an educational tool. Practicing ongoing conversations with this "intelligence," I learn more about how it "thinks" and functions while teaching it new ways of creating or arriving at solutions to various thoughts and problems.

Granted, I'm a nutty person already, so I'm sure I can get AI pretty darned "Stirred" up. But it is just plain fun, at times, to converse with AI and smile, frown, laugh, or giggle at some of the results of our conversations.

I present Volume Two of this little journey, which I've entitled "My Conversations with AI." Come along with me, and let's see what crazy things we may discover by having interesting discussions with artificial intelligence.

Welcome to another stop on our journey to have a "conversation" with AI...

ETIENNE LUTHER

Incredible Fantasy Cliff Houses ???

Being a lifelong student of Art, Architecture, and Design, I decided AI would be an excellent tool to allow me to think outside the proverbial box and create visually stimulating 3D images of fantastic architectural places, potentially pushing the limits of modern-day construction techniques and even the physics involved in making these incredible structures.

This thought process has allowed me to investigate the deepest regions of my imagination to create stunning photorealistic images of places I could have previously only seen in my mind, enabling me to share these visual representations with you.

During my conversations with AI, I proposed this question…

"AI, can you assist me in creating visually stimulating realistic renderings showing incredibly fantastic houses made of various materials that hang onto or are suspended from cliffs or float all by themselves?"

Continuing our collaborative exploration, AI and I delved into the intricacies of design, striving to create compelling images that capture the essence of houses in their unique, precarious settings.

The resulting images on the following pages are graphic representations of several house types, the common denominator being their interrelation with the cliffs or other formations upon which they are constructed.

AI and I curated a select group of images from various architectural styles, utilizing many construction materials. With their distinct features, these images serve as a platform for us and our audience to further our studies, fostering a mutual learning environment. In this process, we also enjoy the freedom to create, unbound by the limitations of our real world, sparking new ideas and pushing the boundaries of our imagination.

Research and studies aside, we can also enjoy viewing these Incredible Fantasy Cliff Houses as visually stimulating images that allow our minds to wonder about the "what ifs…" which is what AI helps us do best.

Table of Contents

<u>Chapter One</u>

Hello, AI, my friend…

Let's discuss incredibly fantastic houses on or around cliffs and their relationship to the ocean.

E T I E N N E   L U T H E R

Chapter Two

Hello, AI, my friend…

Let's discuss incredibly fantastic houses on or around cliffs and the beautiful sunsets we could experience.

Chapter Three

Hello, AI, my friend…

Let's discuss incredibly fantastic houses on or around cliffs built in a cabin or chalet style.

Chapter Four

Hello, AI, my friend…

Let's discuss incredibly fantastic houses on or around cliffs and bodies of water that appear to float.

ETIENNE LUTHER

48

Chapter Five

Hello, AI, my friend…

Let's discuss incredibly fantastic houses suspended from cliffs via cables or other structural supports.

Chapter Six

Hello, AI, my friend…

Let's discuss incredibly fantastic houses built into cave openings in cliffs.

Chapter Seven

Hello, AI, my friend…

Let's discuss incredibly fantastic houses cantilevered on or around cliffs.

I hope you have enjoyed this short stop along our journey to have a "Conversation with AI" about fantastic dwellings that could be constructed and are shown here as fantasy representations of what might become a reality in our future.

As "My Conversations with AI" continues, there is so much to teach, so much to learn, and so little time to answer all our questions about life, love, and the pursuit of happiness, both socially and aesthetically.

Only through our conversations with AI can we begin to scratch the surface of the limitless possibilities it holds. It's not just about finding answers to the questions our minds can fathom; it's about asking new questions and discovering new horizons and frontiers.

If nothing else, we can enjoy the product of our dreams by viewing the outcome of those conversations we continue to have with Artificial Intelligence (AI).

Be on the lookout for more of "My Conversations with AI" books

COMING SOON !

ENJOY...

My Conversations with AI

Volume 2

Incredible Fantasy Cliff Houses ???

A SHORT PICTURE STUDY

THE END

E T I E N N E   L U T H E R